D1190043

Junior Science Books are dedicated to all children who are eager to know more about nature and the world they live in. Written especially for young readers, each Junior Science Book has been carefully tested by the Spache Readability Formula. These books can be read by primary grade children and enjoyed by young readers through the elementary grades.

Junior Science Books are edited and designed under the supervision of
Nancy Larrick, Ed.D.

Junior Science Book of

SOUND

By
Dorothy S. Anderson

Illustrated by Ernest Kurt Barth

**GARRARD
PUBLISHING
COMPANY**
CHAMPAIGN, ILLINOIS

The author and editor are grateful to Dr. James H. Smith, Associate Professor of Physics, University of Illinois, for assistance in checking the accuracy of this book.

Library of Congress Catalog Card Number: 61-9735

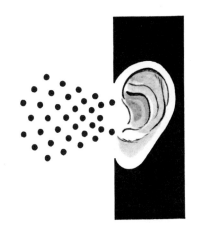

Contents

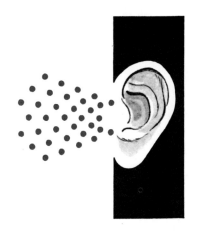

What Are Sounds?

You hear many sounds every day. A jet plane roars across the sky. A balloon bursts. A bat cracks into a baseball. A bee buzzes. People talk.

The sounds seem different. Some are loud. Some are sudden. Some are low. But they all start in the same way.

With a cigar-box violin, you can watch something making a sound. You will need a wooden cigar box and rubber band. Take

off the lid, and slip the rubber band tightly
around the box. Now pull the rubber band
out. Let it go suddenly. You will hear a
humming sound. But what do you see?

Take a close look. The rubber band
looks wider than before. It is shaking. It
is moving back and forth very, very fast.

We call this movement *vibration*. We
say that the rubber band *vibrates* when
it moves this way. We call the rubber
band the *vibrator*.

When you find more rubber bands, save them for your cigar-box violin. You will need them with other experiments.

Everything that makes a sound vibrates. Strings inside a piano vibrate. A bell vibrates when it is struck.

You can't always see the vibrations as you could with the rubber band. But sometimes you can feel the vibrations.

Put your fingers lightly on your throat. Now read the next sentence out loud. You will feel the vibrations of your vocal cords.

When something stops vibrating, the sound it makes stops too. You can see this if you hold a metal pan lid by its handle.

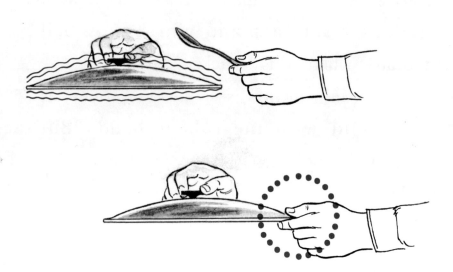

Hit the edge lightly with a spoon. The lid will ring. Now grip the edge tightly. The vibrations stop. The sound has stopped too. If there are no vibrations, there will be no sound.

A drum player knows this. When he strikes the drum, it vibrates. The vibrations

With his hand he stops the vibrations.

cause the sound. When he wants his drum
to stop sounding, he holds his hand on it.
This stops the vibrations.

Scientists have studied some of the
interesting sounds in nature. They want
to know what vibrates to make the sounds.

They studied the cricket. He seems to
sing without opening his mouth at all. His
song does not come from a vibration in
his throat.

Instead, he holds his front wings over his back. As they touch, he rubs them together. Each front wing has a rough edge with many teeth sticking up from it. These teeth vibrate when he scratches the wings together. They make the cricket's song.

You can make a sound somewhat the same way. Rub two combs together. As the teeth of the combs vibrate, you hear a sound.

What about the rattle of a rattlesnake?

A snake is always growing a new skin. When a rattlesnake crawls out of his old skin, a ring of that skin stays on his tail. The rings of old skins harden. They become the rattles.

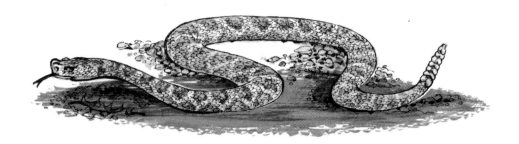

When the rattlesnake is angry, he throws this tail quickly to one side. The rattles hit against each other. They vibrate and make the rattling sound.

What about the hum of bees? When bees are very busy, their hive gives off a humming sound. But the bees do not hum in their throats as we do. They are busy cooling the honey to make it ripe. They do this by fanning their wings up and down. The wings go up and down as many as 18,000 times every minute. These vibrating wings make the humming sound.

All the sounds we hear come from vibrations. Sometimes you can see the vibrations. Sometimes you can feel them. Some vibrations have a regular motion like a grandfather's clock. Others are sudden like a big blast. When the vibrations stop, the sound stops too.

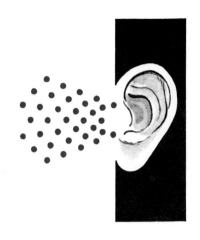

How Sound Travels

Did you ever toss a pebble into a quiet pond? What happened to the water? Tiny waves rolled away from the place where the pebble dropped. The waves were in circles.

You can see the same thing in a sink full of water. Wet your finger and let the water become still. Then shake your hand so that a drop falls on the water. Tiny waves will roll away in circles.

13

Sound travels in waves also. When something vibrates, air waves go off in all directions. We call them sound waves.

You can see how a sound wave travels. Find a long rope. Have a friend hold one end while you hold the other. Pull the rope out tight. While your friend holds his end still, shake your end up and down rapidly. You will see a wave travel over the rope. Your hand is the

You can see how a wave travels over the rope.

vibrator that starts the wave moving.

Remember the rubber band and the wooden box? When the rubber band vibrated, it pushed the air. It started a sound wave.

What happens when a sound wave goes through air? Do this experiment with a row of dominoes. Stand each domino upright on its smallest end. When you have a long row, push the first domino over.

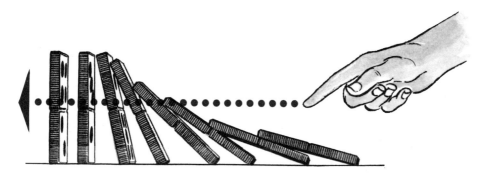

Each domino pushes the next one over.

It will push the next one over. That will push the next one over. Finally, the whole row will be pushed over. Sound waves travel through air in somewhat the same way.

Everything is made of many tiny bits, called *molecules*. When the rubber band vibrates, it pushes the air molecules next to it. These molecules push their neighbors. These, in turn, push the next ones.

Sound waves go through the air in all directions. They go up, down, around corners, and out on all sides. You can hear the sound of a jet plane above you. And you can hear voices from the basement below you.

Sound waves travel through other things besides air. They will travel through wood, metal, the ground, and many other things. Anything that carries a sound is called a sound *conductor*.

Most of the time we hear through air. That is because our ears are usually next

16

to air. They are not often next to something hard like wood.

Sound travels through hard conductors the same way it travels through air.

Try listening through some hard sound conductors. Put an alarm clock at one end of a wooden bench. Or put it at one end of a board five feet long. Place your ear at the opposite end. You will hear the ticking through the wood.

An iron railing is another good conductor. Put your ear at one end while a friend taps the other end. The tap will travel through the iron to your ear.

You can make a string telephone to carry sound. You will need two paper cups and a string the length of a room. Make a pinhole in the bottom of each cup. Pull one end of the string through one cup. Tie a knot inside the cup so the other end will not slip out. Do the same for the other cup. Now pull the cups apart until the string is tight.

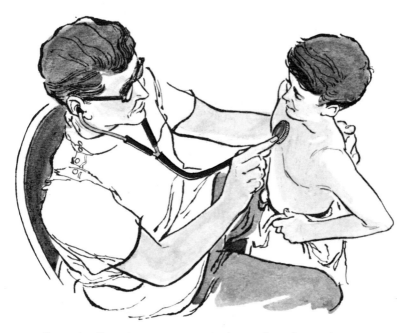

Sound vibrations are carried to the doctor's ear.

Don't let the string touch anything between the cups. If you have the string going through a doorway, don't let the string touch the wall. Hold one cup to your ear, while a friend whispers into the other cup. The whisper will sound very close.

The doctor listens to your breathing in much the same way. He uses a special instrument called a *stethoscope*. The small flat disk picks up the sound vibrations in your chest. These vibrations cause the molecules of air in the tubes to vibrate. The vibrations of the molecules are then carried to the doctor's ear.

Indians used to listen to sound waves through the ground. They would put an ear to the ground. They could hear far-away hoofbeats.

Try this experiment to see how the Indians heard their messages. Put your ear to the ground at one end of the yard. Have a friend gallop toward you from the opposite end of the yard. You will hear the gallop through the ground.

When someone in the same room speaks, you hear the sound at once. What about sound from far away? Many times, of course, distant sounds die down before they reach us.

What about very loud sounds? Try this

Indians used to listen to sound waves through the ground.

experiment. Have a friend stand at the end of a long block and beat a drum. Watch his hand carefully. You will see him hit the drum *before* you hear the sound. The sound takes some time to reach you.

Sound travels a little more than 1,000 feet in one second. Light travels much

You will see the lightning before you hear thunder.

faster. That is why you see the drum being beaten first. Later you hear the sound.

Remember this during the next thunderstorm. You will see the lightning. Then you will hear the thunder. They happen at the same time. But light waves travel faster than sound waves.

You can figure out how far the lightning was from you. When you first see the lightning, count, "One thousand-one, one thousand-two, one thousand-three . . . "

Keep counting until you hear the sound of thunder. If you count up to one thousand-five, for example, it took five seconds for the sound to reach you.

You know that sound travels at about 1,000 feet in one second. In five seconds, the sound traveled 5,000 feet. The lightning was 5,000 feet from you.

For many years men thought that airplanes could never go faster than sound. When airplanes traveled almost as fast as sound, they were hard to control. Men thought there was a "sound barrier."

Now, however, jets travel much faster than the speed of sound. We say, "They have broken the sound barrier."

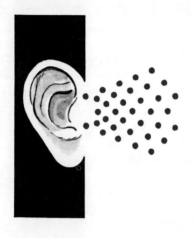

Inside Your Ear

When the speaker of a radio vibrates, sound waves go out in all directions. If you are near by, some of them strike your ears. Then interesting things begin to happen.

Inside each ear, there is a thin piece of skin or membrane. It is called the eardrum because it is stretched tight like the top of a drum.

When sound waves hit your eardrum, it vibrates. This vibration is carried to the brain. There you think about the sound and figure out what caused it.

Try this experiment. Hold a piece of cardboard near a loud radio. You can feel the cardboard vibrate. That is the way your eardrum vibrates when sound hits it.

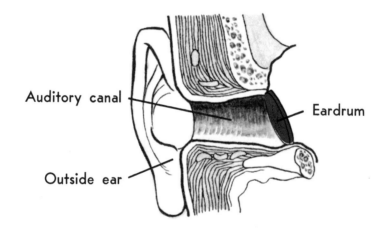

Dogs and cats have ears something like ours. But they can hear some sounds we can't hear. Watch a dog with his ears perked up. Perhaps he is listening to something that you cannot hear. That's because a dog can hear higher sounds than we can.

The rabbit uses his long ears to help him catch sound waves. He holds his ears up, especially when he fears danger.

You can try this. Hold your hand behind your ear and turn to a noise. Take your hand down, and you will not hear the noise so well.

Katydids and crickets have ears on their front legs. Frog ears have the eardrum out on the frog's skin.

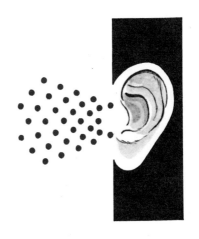

Where Does the Sound Come From?

When we decide where sounds come from, we are usually guessing. Sometimes our guesses are right. Sometimes they are wrong.

You try this experiment with a friend. Blindfold him. Have him sit quietly. Ask him to point to the noises he hears.

Perhaps a watch is ticking somewhere. Perhaps someone is walking on the floor overhead. Toss some paper across the room to make a noise. Be careful that your friend doesn't hear you moving.

See if he can tell where the sounds come from.

Probably your friend will move his head as he guesses. The move may be so slight that you can't see it. He turns his head to see how the sounds hit each ear. You do this, too, when you guess where sounds come from.

When sound comes from one side, it reaches the ear on that side sooner than the other ear. Your brain notes this small difference. It tells you from which direction the sound came.

Sometimes a sound seems louder at your right ear than at your left. When that happens, you usually turn your head toward the right. You turn your head

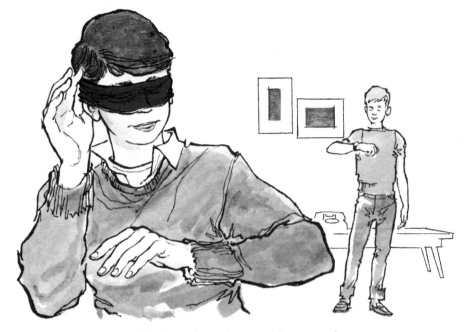

He turns his head to locate the sound.

until the sounds seem the same to both ears. Then you decide the sound is coming from the direction you are facing.

If your ears were not shaped in the way they are, you would not be able to tell if a sound comes from in front or in back of you. But your ears are shaped to make a difference in the distance the sound must travel. This helps you decide if the sound comes from the front or from behind.

Scientists tried an interesting experiment on this. They made a blindfolded person sit without moving. They used special equipment to make sure he could not move his head. Then they set a watch ticking at the same distance from both ears. The blindfolded person couldn't tell where the sound came from.

When we guess where a sound comes from, we depend on many things.

Habit helps us. We recognize a cat's meowing. So we look toward the floor. When we hear a bird singing, we guess the sound comes from a tree. Suppose you hear a car. If you know a driveway is near by, you guess the sound comes from there.

By habit, we connect certain sounds with certain places. But sometimes it is hard to know where a sound comes from.

On a dark evening, take the shade from a table lamp and turn on the light bulb. Light waves go out in all directions.

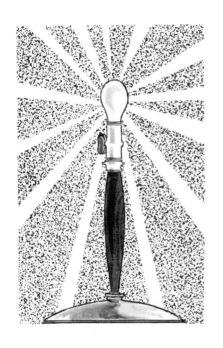

Place an empty coffee can over the light bulb. The light waves are directed down toward the table.

Now stand blindfolded in a room with a friend. If he whispers your name,

31

you can hear it. But you may not be able to tell where he is standing. If he whispers your name through a megaphone, it is easier to tell where he is standing. The megaphone directs the sound waves toward you. It acts like the coffee can over the light bulb. The coffee can directed the light waves toward the table.

Often your eyes help you guess where sounds come from. When we hear a voice, we look to *see* who is speaking. But our eyes can fool us too.

If you see someone moving his lips, you think he is speaking. You may be wrong though.

Think of a ventriloquist and his dummy. The ventriloquist can talk without moving his lips. He makes the sounds. At the same time, he makes the dummy's lips move. The dummy seems to speak.

The voice seems to come from the dummy.

When we hear the voice, we look at the dummy. His lips are moving. So we think he is talking. The sound seems to come from the dummy, even when we know it isn't.

The same thing happens at the movies. The voices seem to come from the actors on the screen. Actually, the voices are coming from the sound track. That may be somewhere behind our heads. Just the same, we think the voices are coming from the actors on the screen.

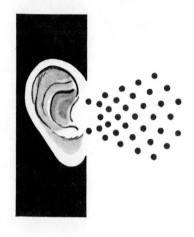

Resonance

Hold a seashell to your ear. Do you hear a roaring sound? Some people say it is like the roar of the sea.

What you hear is not really the sea, of course. You hear the same sound without a seashell. Make the shape of a hollow box with your hands. Hold your hands close to one ear. Listen carefully. You hear the roaring sound again.

When air is kept in a small space, it

catches sounds from the outside. The air starts to vibrate along with some noises outside. We say it is in *resonance* with the outside noise.

Do you play the piano? Is there a lamp shade in the same room? Perhaps the lamp shade started to rattle while you played. Probably the rattle disturbed you, and you moved the shade around a bit to stop it.

Next time try this experiment before you stop the rattle. Go back and play each piano key by itself. You will find one particular key that starts the lamp shade rattling. The lamp shade is in resonance with the piano key. Sometimes the rattle comes from a picture frame near by.

Each sound wave has a size. Sometimes a nearby object can make sound waves the same size. Suppose the sound waves from the piano meet that object. If their sound waves match, the object will begin to vibrate too. We say it is in resonance with the piano.

One note on the piano sent out a wave that fit the sound waves of the lamp shade. This wave began to move the shade along with it. Finally the shade vibrated by itself. In the same way, the air in your cupped hand was in resonance with some outside sound.

The seashell seems to give a roaring sound.

Try this experiment. Hold down the sustaining pedal of your piano. Then sing a note while holding down the pedal. When you stop singing, you will hear a humming sound from the piano. The sound comes from the piano string which is in resonance with your voice.

Resonance is not unusual. Most sounds have other sounds in resonance with them. In fact, resonance often makes the first sound more pleasant. Sounds from violin strings would be weak by themselves. But the air inside the violin box is in resonance. This makes the sounds stronger and more beautiful.

Resonance is like getting into swing with something else. Imagine a friend swinging low on a swing. If you want to push him higher, you cannot push just any old way. You have to go forward and back just the way the swing is moving. You get in swing. Being in swing to push someone is like being in resonance with another sound. One sound wave pushes another thing until the second thing is sounding too.

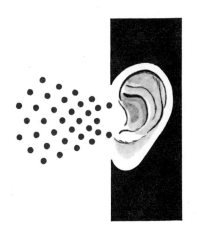

Outdoor Echoes

Did you ever shout across to a mountain-side and hear an echo? It sounds like a voice shouting back. Long ago people thought the echo was some magic person.

You can get an echo in the city too. Stand at least 55 feet from a brick or stone wall. Shout toward the wall. Then you will hear the echo.

It is a sound wave that bounced from the wall.

Sailors use echoes to tell distance.

Sailors use echoes from mountainous shores. In foggy weather the echoes are very useful. Sometimes the sailors want to find out if they are near the shore. They call out loudly. They count the time until the echo comes back. If it takes a long time, they know they are far from shore. A quick echo means the mountainous shore is near.

Sailors also use echoes to tell how deep the sea is. The instrument they use is called a depth finder. This sends a sound down into the sea. The depth finder measures the time it takes for an echo to come back. This tells how deep the sea is at that point. With depth finders, men can make maps of the floor of the ocean.

Sometimes men can find oil by using echoes. They make a small hole in the ground. Then they set off dynamite in the hole. From this, sound waves travel down through the ground. When the sound waves strike a layer of rock, an echo travels back to the surface. Oil men find how long it takes for the echo to come back. This tells them what kind of rock lies below. Sometimes they can tell if it is an oil-bearing rock and how far down it lies.

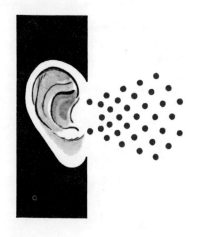

Bouncing Echoes

Outdoor sound waves bounce back and make echoes. In a closed room sound waves can bounce, too. That is, they will bounce if the walls are flat and hard.

Usually we don't hear distinct echoes in a closed room. We don't hear them because the walls aren't far enough apart. The sound waves bounce from one wall to another and make a roaring sound. We call this *reverberation*.

When someone talks in a new auditorium, the sounds sometimes reverberate. The room seems noisy. After the speaker starts, the roaring begins. This makes it hard to hear what he is saying. People say the auditorium has poor *acoustics*.

You can make the acoustics better. Draperies can be hung about the room. Carpets can be put down. A curtain can be put across the stage. These things make the walls and floor softer and the surfaces uneven. Soft, uneven surfaces will swallow up the sound waves.

Perhaps you have been in a new house where there is no furniture. Maybe you have been in an old, deserted one that is empty. Sometimes people say a new house sounds empty. They say an old, deserted house sounds spooky.

You can guess what happens. There

are no rugs or draperies or furniture to swallow up the sound waves. So the sounds echo and hum about.

If someone puts up curtains and lays rugs on the floor, you hear no echo. They swallow the sound waves. There are not so many reverberations. The house seems cozier.

We have special material which will swallow up sound waves. It is used for walls and ceilings. It is soft and has many small holes like a sponge.

Look for sound-proof material in public buildings. Perhaps the ceiling of a restaurant has it. Maybe you can see it on the walls or ceiling of an auditorium. Perhaps you can find a music room or a music practicing room which has it. Perhaps you can see it in a telephone booth.

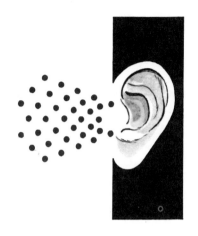

Loud and Soft — High and Low

Tap your finger lightly on a door. Now rap on the door. One sound is quiet, and the other is loud. The more strength you use, the louder the sound is.

If you hit piano keys hard, you make a loud sound. If you press the keys down lightly, the music is soft.

Try to make a loud sound on your cigar-box violin. Then make a soft sound.

Notice what you do. The more strength you put into making a sound, the louder the sound will be.

When you make a loud sound, look at the rubber band. Now look at it when you make a soft sound. You will see that the rubber band swings out farther with the loud sound. It doesn't swing out so much for a soft sound.

The same things happen when a bell rings loudly and when a bell rings softly. If you swing a bell hard, the clapper hits

The clapper makes the bell vibrate.

the bell with a great deal of force. Then the bell vibrates with wide swings. If you swing the bell gently, the clapper hits gently. The bell vibrates with small swings.

Also, some sounds are high and other sounds are low. We call the highness of a sound its *pitch*. When you sing different notes in a song, you sing different pitches.

Put several rubber bands around your cigar-box violin. Be sure one rubber band is fat and another is thin. Pluck the fat rubber band. You hear a low strum. Play

The thin rubber band gives a higher note.

the thin rubber band. It makes a higher sound.

Now pull one rubber band tightly around the box. Then play it. It gives a high note. Now loosen the rubber band and play it. The sound is lower when the rubber band is loose.

A thin, tight string or rubber band usually gives a high pitch. A thick, loose string or rubber band usually gives a low pitch. This is because thinner, tighter strings tend to vibrate faster. Also, a short string vibrates faster than a long one.

Inside a piano, there are many different strings. Some are long. Some are short. Some are thicker than others. Some have been made tighter by the piano tuner.

When you play the piano, you cause little hammers to hit these strings. Then the strings vibrate and make the different notes.

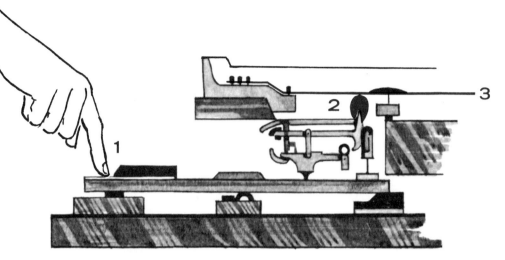

This cross-section picture shows how a piano key works. The player strikes the key (No. 1). This makes the hammer (No. 2) strike the string (No. 3).

There is a string for every note. The keys on the right of a piano give a high pitch. Keys at the left give a lower pitch.

A violin has only four strings. How can a violinist get so many musical notes?

Watch a violinist play. When his finger holds down a string, the vibrating part is shorter. That gives a higher pitch. If the violinist moves his finger just a little way up, the sound is still higher. By moving his

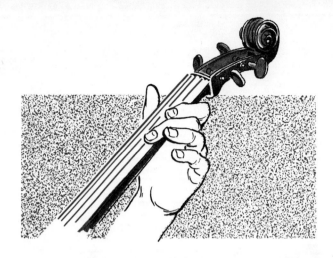

fingers to different positions, he can play the whole scale.

Many musical instruments have strings which start the sound waves. The harp is one. The cello, guitar, mandolin, and viola have strings, too.

STRINGED INSTRUMENTS

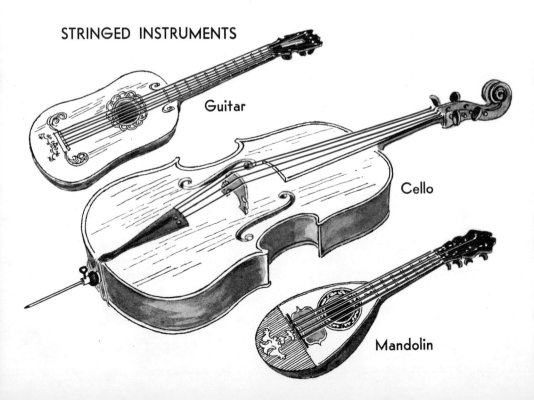

Guitar

Cello

Mandolin

Pipes and horns make their sounds a different way. They use air to start the sound waves. You can see how this works.

Use a pop bottle for your experiment. Put your bottom lip level with the mouth of the bottle. Bring your upper lip down until your lips are almost closed. Blow a gentle, steady stream of air. Try to aim it at the opposite edge of the bottle mouth. Blow until a note comes from the bottle.

There are no strings to vibrate. You cannot see anything vibrating. What makes the sound? It is the air inside the bottle. Your breath has made it vibrate. This vibrating column of air makes the sound you hear.

Remember how the violinist changed pitch by shortening his strings? You can change pitch by shortening the column of air.

Put some water into the bottle. Fill it about halfway up. Now blow a note. The sound is higher because the column of air is shorter.

Add more water, and blow another note. It has a higher pitch than the last.

The shorter the column of air, the higher the pitch.

Here is another experiment. Get some soda straws. Blow softly into the top of a straw until you have a note. Now make the column of air shorter by cutting off an inch of the straw. Blow again. The pitch will be higher than your first one. Keep cutting off the straw an inch at a time. Each time blow a note. The pitch is higher each time.

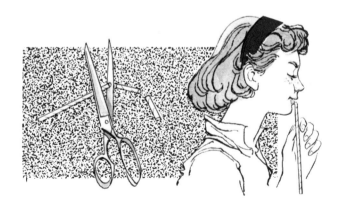

Many musical instruments have a vibrating column of air. Some of them are the flute, the oboe, the saxophone, the recorder, and the trumpet.

The flute has holes down the side. The flute player covers certain holes with his fingers. This makes the air column longer or shorter.

These musical instruments are called wind instruments because each one has a column of air.

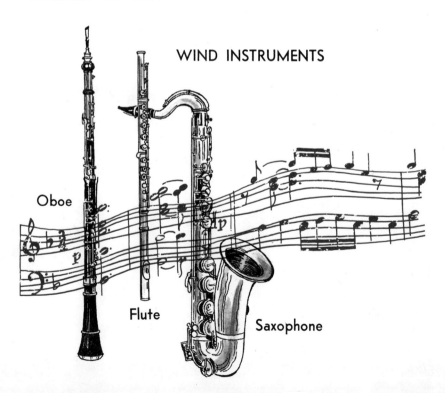

WIND INSTRUMENTS

Oboe

Flute

Saxophone

A xylophone has many wooden bars of different lengths.

The xylophone has no strings and no columns of air. It has many wooden bars. They are of different lengths. You strike the bars to make the sounds. Long bars make low notes. Short bars make high notes.

Chimes and bells are of different sizes too. You can see how these instruments work.

Collect 10 glass bottles of different sizes. Cut strings of different lengths, and tie them to the bottle necks.

Find a narrow piece of wood or a long, strong stick. Balance it over the backs of two chairs. Tie the bottles onto the stick. Arrange them so they do not hit against each other. You may have to shorten or lengthen some of the strings.

When the bottles are hanging freely, tap the bottom of each with a spoon. Listen to the pitch of each bottle. The short bottles give high notes. The long bottles give low notes.

Arrange the high-pitched bottles at one end, and the low-pitched bottles at the other end. Now play a tune on your bottle xylophone. Add more bottles until you have the pitches you want.

In chimes, big bells give low notes. The little bells give high notes. Each bell has a pitch. The pitch depends on the shape, the size, and the weight of the bell.

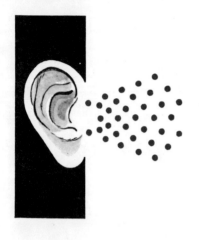

When You Speak

When you speak, you move your mouth. You move other things too. Your throat, your nose, the back of your mouth, and your lungs are all used in speaking. They work together like a musical instrument.

There is a voice box down in your throat. Two thick cords are stretched across it. They are called *vocal cords*.

The voice box acts something like a stringed instrument. The lungs send air up to the voice box. The air blows between the vocal cords and makes them vibrate. Put your fingers lightly to your throat. When you speak, you can feel your vocal cords vibrating.

You make some changes in your vocal cords when you speak. You do this without thinking about it. Sometimes you make the vocal cords stretch tight. Then your voice sounds high pitched. Sometimes you let vocal cords become loose. Then your voice is low pitched.

Probably you know someone whose voice croaked during a cold. For a day or two, his voice sounded strange. The vocal cords were swollen. They vibrated so slowly that the person's voice was low pitched.

The vocal cords do not vibrate for all sounds. Say *Fff* and *Vee*. Can you tell any difference between them? You make them very much alike. The difference is that you use your vocal cords for *Vee*, but not for *Fff*. Put your fingers lightly on your throat when you say these sounds. Then you can tell the difference.

Every day you say about 41 different sounds. It took you years to learn how to say all these sounds. You practiced them a long time. Now you say them without thinking about them.

Try these sounds: *Puh, Ssss, Mmmm.*

When you say *Puh,* you send air from your mouth. The air goes out through your lips with a tiny explosion. When you say *Ssss,* you use your tongue and teeth and make a hissing sound. You change the shape of your mouth to say different sounds.

When you say *Mmmm,* you close your mouth. You make a sound that resonates up in your nose. Your nose and mouth act like wind instruments.

Speech sounds are made in many different ways. And there are many kinds of sounds. Yet all the sounds start in the same way. Something vibrates and sends out sound waves.

Index

ABOUT THE AUTHOR

DOROTHY S. ANDERSON became interested in the subject of sound when she was a graduate student at Boston University. While taking a course on teaching science in the elementary school, she found few books had been written for children about sound. She determined to write a book that would give accurate information about sound and that would be simple enough for young readers. *The Junior Science Book of Sound* is the result. Her stories, articles and plays for children have appeared in many magazines, including *Child Life, Calling All Girls, Instructor* and *Grade Teacher.*

For four years Mrs. Anderson taught in the elementary school. Since then she has taught at Boston's International Institute and the Boston Center for Adult Education.

She lives in Boston with her husband, who is a lawyer, and their two children.

ABOUT THE ARTIST

ERNEST KURT BARTH, a native New Yorker, studied art at Pratt Institute in Brooklyn. For several years he gave full time to commercial art for advertising. But his own love of reading and his interest in beautiful books soon turned him to book illustrations.

He has illustrated many children's books, including *The Golden Fleece, All About Great Medical Discoveries,* and a recent edition of *Gulliver's Travels.*